Ri... Little Word Book

Random House 🏠 New York

First American Edition. Copyright © 1978 by Richard Scarry. All rights reserved under International and Pan-American Copyright Conventions. Published in the United States by Random House, Inc., New York, and simultaneously in Canada by Random House of Canada Limited, Toronto. Originally published in Great Britain as *Richard Scarry's Busy-busy Word Book* by William Collins Sons & Co. Ltd., Glasgow and London. Copyright © 1977 by William Collins Sons & Co. Ltd. ISBN: 0-394-83964-1. *Library of Congress Catalog Card Number:* 78-55301.
Manufactured in the United States of America   1 2 3 4 5 6 7 8 9 0

sailboat

Sam Pig

rowboat

hammer

cap

oar

oarsman

three men in a tub

flag

ocean liner

sailor

Help!

submarine

saw

toolbox

clothing factory

rolls of cloth

table

paper patterns

tailor needle

sewing machine

buttons

thimble

scissors

pieces of cloth

seamstress

dress

dresses

rack

trees

truck

nursemaid

tricycle

fire
hydrant

line painter

NEWS STAND

newspapers

sign

cars

NO PARKING

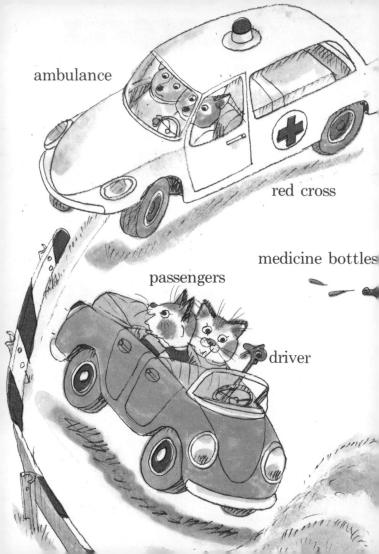

ambulance

red cross

medicine bottles

passengers

driver

mail truck

MAIL

hat

instruments

doctor's car

M.D.

bumpy road

coach

All aboard!

lamp

signalman

travelers

cart

motorists

milk can

milkman

driver

engine

motorcycle

policeman

apple

exhaust

log transporter

tree

stump

branches

three tramps

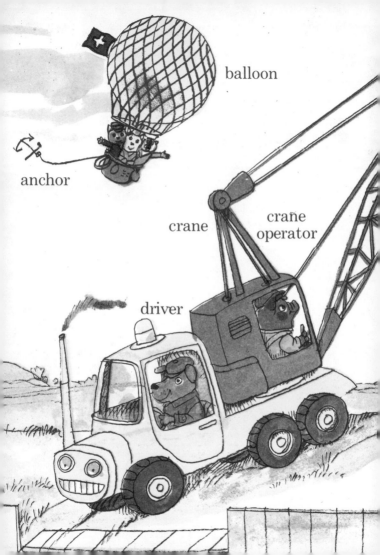

balloon

anchor

crane

crane
operator

driver

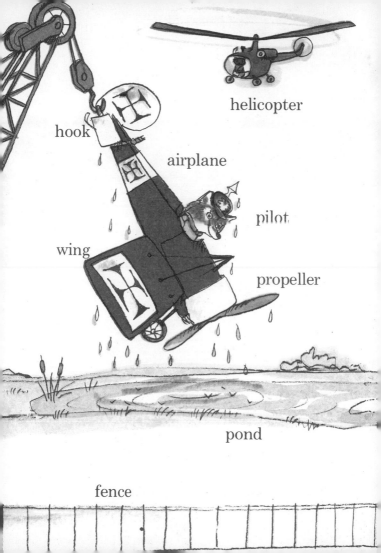

helicopter

hook

airplane

pilot

wing

propeller

pond

fence

cuckoo clock

cook's hat

ketchup

apron

cook

cookbook

can opener

pickle

can

rack

door

keyhole

mouse

kitchen utensils

saucepan

kettle

meat

frying pan

stove

bucket

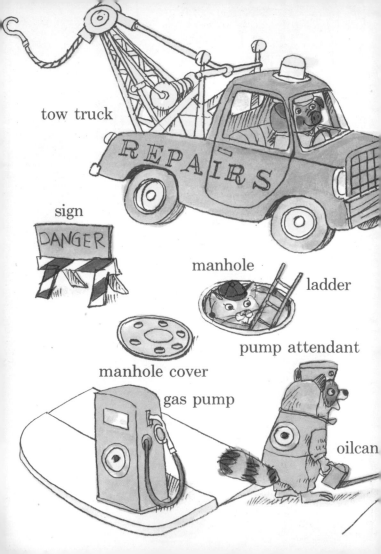

tow truck

REPAIRS

sign

DANGER

manhole

ladder

pump attendant

manhole cover

gas pump

oilcan

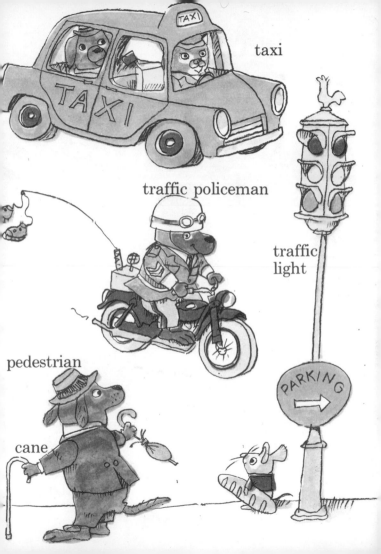

taxi

traffic policeman

traffic light

pedestrian

cane

hay

hat

farmer

hay cart

wheels

tractor

sanitation truck

REFUSE REMOVAL

flat tire

jack

helmet

racing car

truck driver

letters

MAIL

AIR MAIL

mail truck

tears

baby

baby
carriage

airliner

SWISSAIR

fuel tank

jets

sleeping mechanic

ladder

radar nose

landing gear

luggage carts

fuel tanker

Little Ben's bag

Daddy's bag

Mommy's bag

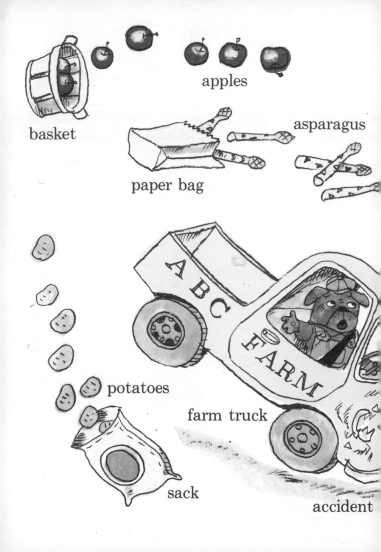

apples

basket

asparagus

paper bag

potatoes

farm truck

sack

accident

tools

emergency stop

Father Cat

hat

tramp

crowded car

tow
truck

broken-
down
car

a muddy road

Father Pig

sun

hammer

cloud

bolt

Huckle

Lowly

spring

engine trouble

a sinking car

SPEE
LIMIT
60
M.P.H.

shopper

traffic island

mouse driver

mouse car

GAR AND BAGE

garbage can

sanitation truck

chimney pots

mail truck

pedestrian

BANK

barred window

sidewalk

banana peel

fruit

mother cat

little
cat

scooter

lollipop

drinking
straw

table

chair

diner

THREE STAR
RESTAURANT

REST
ROO

car

wheelbarrow

train

dining car

mailbags

traveler

mouse in
a
hurry

porter   luggage wagon

DIESEL ELECTRIC LOCOMOTIVE

FUEL OIL

oil-can

diesel fuel tank

railwayman

TRACK 2

buffers

rails

newspaper

passenger

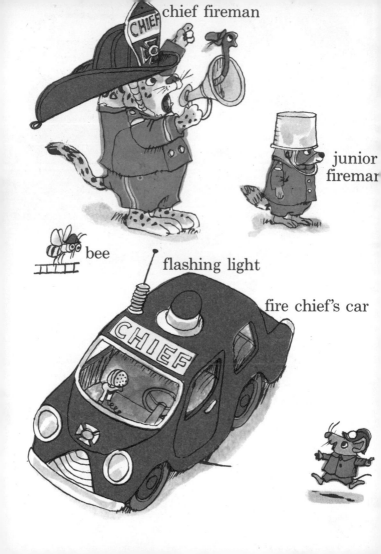

chief fireman

junior fireman

bee

flashing light

fire chief's car

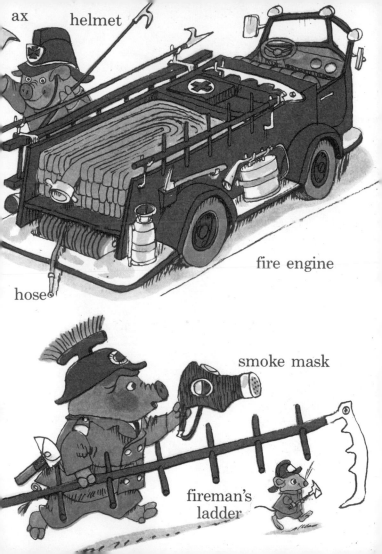

ax

helmet

fire engine

hose

smoke mask

fireman's ladder

dustpan

pea pod

turnip

tomatoes

lettuce

potatoes

garlic

pomegranate

asparagus

carrots

spinach

cabbage

shopkeeper

watermelon

pepper

soap

sponge

brush

pail

lemon

celery

basket of eggs

pineapple

runaway car

flag

flagpole

DRINK WATER

blimp

clothesline

path

grass

roller skater

South →

road signs

STOP

NO ENTRY

5

DANGER

SIGNS

roller skates

mad motorist

angry farmer

road worker

barrier

bolt

nut

weather vane

chimneys

rooftops

village street

aviator

glove

monoplane

houses

antique car

tarpaulin

wheel

truck

banana peel

road sweeper

pie

sunroof

license
plate

man at work

minicar

hole
in
the
road

road drill

musical firemen

drum

trombone

cement mixer

suitcase

Huckle

Uncle
Willie

a rough road

antique car

wrench

mop

plumber's
truck

PLUMBER

taxi

TAXI

police car

POLICE

unusual car

BANANA · MOBILE

NUT

bicycle

ice cream vendor

ICE CREAM

customers

sleepy mouse

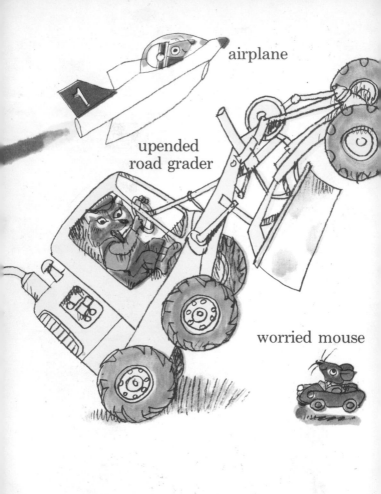

airplane

upended
road grader

worried mouse